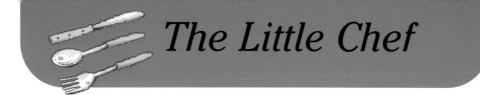

The Little Chef

Fun Party Food
Little Chef Recipes

Author: Mercedes Segarra
Illustrations: Rosa M. Curto

Enslow Elementary
an imprint of

E **Enslow Publishers, Inc.**
40 Industrial Road
Box 398
Berkeley Heights, NJ 07922
USA

http://www.enslow.com

Before You Start Cooking

1 Wash your hands with soap before you start working.

2 Wear an apron so your clothes will not get dirty.

3 If you have long hair, you can tie it back so it will not bother you while you cook, and no hair will fall into the food.

4 Before you start, read the recipe. Make sure you have all the necessary ingredients, and follow instructions step-by-step.

5 Weigh and measure all ingredients before you start cooking.

6 **Ask an adult** to help you turn on the oven or to cut ingredients with a sharp knife or scissors.

7 If you need to use the burners on the stove, please **ask an adult** to help you, too.

8 If you need to use the oven, it is a good idea to turn it on just as you begin the recipe so it will be hot when you finally need it.

9 Turn off the stove or the oven when you have finished using it.

3

10 Use pot holders to take pots, pans, or trays off the stove or out of the oven so you will not burn your hands.

11 Move the pot handles out of the way so you do not knock into them accidentally and drop them or burn yourself.

12 Clean the utensils as you cook. When you are done cooking, leave the kitchen as tidy as you found it.

Pancakes with Whipped Cream

4

Ingredients:

1/2 cup of all-purpose flour

1 3/4 tablespoons of sugar

2 eggs

1 3/4 tablespoons of butter

1 cup of milk

a dash of salt

You can also serve the pancakes with hot fudge, jam, honey, or ice cream.

1 Put flour, sugar, eggs, milk, and salt in a bowl.

2 Mix the ingredients until you get a very thin batter.

3 Melt a teaspoon of butter in a hot pan. Pour two or three tablespoons of batter into the pan.

4 Cook the thin pancake on both sides until golden.

5 Put two tablespoons of whipped cream on a pancake and roll it. Repeat.

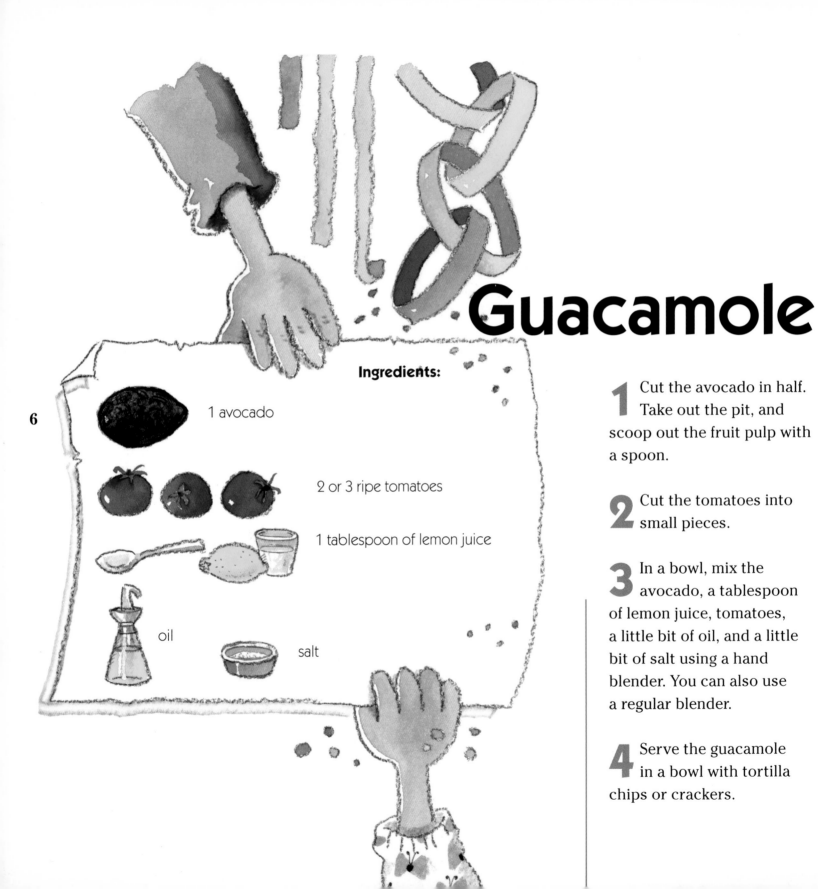

Guacamole

6

Ingredients:

1 avocado

2 or 3 ripe tomatoes

1 tablespoon of lemon juice

oil

salt

1 Cut the avocado in half. Take out the pit, and scoop out the fruit pulp with a spoon.

2 Cut the tomatoes into small pieces.

3 In a bowl, mix the avocado, a tablespoon of lemon juice, tomatoes, a little bit of oil, and a little bit of salt using a hand blender. You can also use a regular blender.

4 Serve the guacamole in a bowl with tortilla chips or crackers.

7

Tomato and Mozzarella Skewers

Ingredients:

cherry tomatoes

mozzarella

wooden skewers

16 fresh basil leaves

olive oil

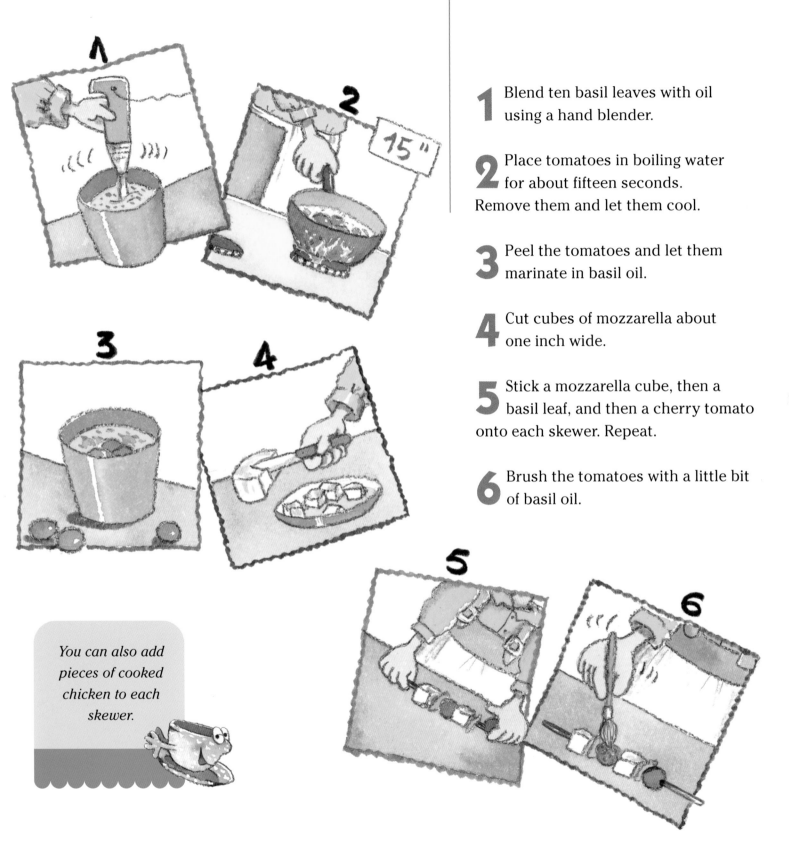

1 Blend ten basil leaves with oil using a hand blender.

2 Place tomatoes in boiling water for about fifteen seconds. Remove them and let them cool.

3 Peel the tomatoes and let them marinate in basil oil.

4 Cut cubes of mozzarella about one inch wide.

5 Stick a mozzarella cube, then a basil leaf, and then a cherry tomato onto each skewer. Repeat.

6 Brush the tomatoes with a little bit of basil oil.

You can also add pieces of cooked chicken to each skewer.

9

Ingredients:

1 sheet of puff pastry

2 or 3 ripe tomatoes

pesto sauce

a dash of salt

Puff Pastry with Tomato and Pesto

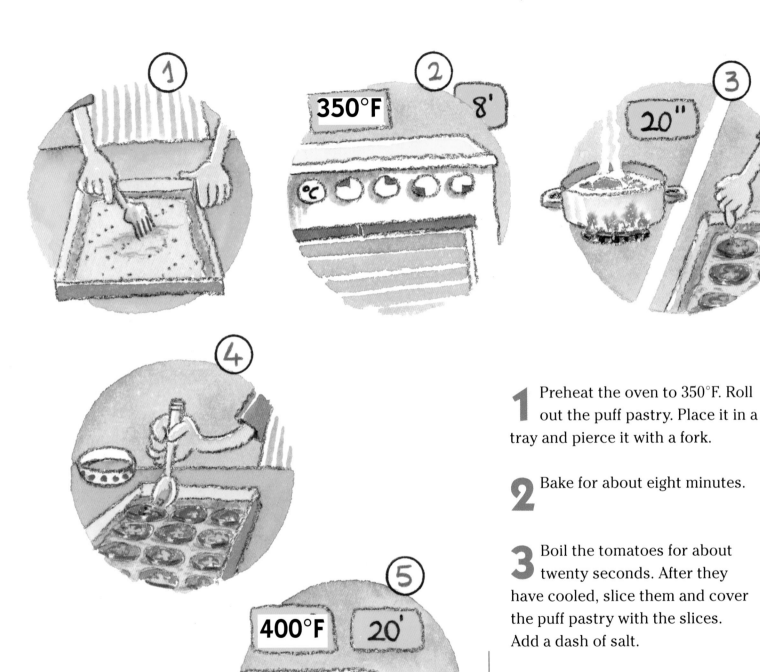

1 Preheat the oven to 350°F. Roll out the puff pastry. Place it in a tray and pierce it with a fork.

2 Bake for about eight minutes.

3 Boil the tomatoes for about twenty seconds. After they have cooled, slice them and cover the puff pastry with the slices. Add a dash of salt.

4 Sprinkle the tomatoes with the pesto sauce.

5 Bake again for about twenty minutes at 400°F.

Ingredients:

4 chicken breasts

2 eggs

bread crumbs

oil

salt

You may serve the chicken nuggets with different dipping sauces, such as ketchup, honey mustard, ranch, etc.

Chicken Nuggets

1 Cut the chicken breasts into cubes.

2 Beat the eggs until you get a frothy mix.

3 Place the chicken cubes in the egg. Let them marinate in the refrigerator for about half an hour.

4 Heat oil in a frying pan.

5 Add salt to the bread crumbs. Roll each chicken cube in the bread crumbs.

6 When the oil in the pan is hot, fry the nuggets until they are golden. Make sure they are cooked all the way through.

Summer Pie

Ingredients:

1 loaf of regular sandwich bread (no crust)

2 cans of tuna

3 tomatoes

green olives

mayonnaise

1 teaspoon of sugar

a dash of salt

1 Grate the tomatoes and add a teaspoon of sugar and a dash of salt.

2 Cook the tomatoes over medium heat for seven minutes until you get a sauce.

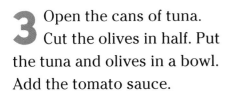

3 Open the cans of tuna. Cut the olives in half. Put the tuna and olives in a bowl. Add the tomato sauce.

4 Add a tablespoon and a half of mayonnaise and mix well.

5 In a loaf pan, place a layer of slices of bread. Cover it with half the mixture. Next, add another layer of bread slices, and cover it again with the rest of the mixture.

6 Finally, put a top layer of bread slices. Refrigerate the pie for about six hours.

Popcorn Balls

Ingredients:

1/2 cup of unpopped popcorn kernels

1/3 cup of butter

3/4 cup of sugar

2 tablespoons of heavy cream

1 tablespoon of honey

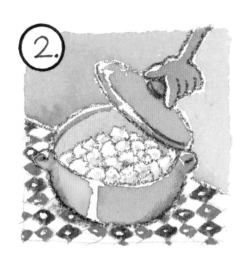

1 Heat oil in a pan. Add the kernels and cover the pan with a tight lid.

2 Shake the pan once in a while, holding the lid in place. Remove it from the heat when the popcorn stops popping.

3 In a smaller pan, heat the sugar, butter, honey, and cream until the sugar melts. Let the mix boil for about five minutes. Keep stirring it to keep it from burning.

4 Pour the caramel mixture over the popcorn. Mix it well with a metal spoon.

5 Let it cool. Oil your hands and make popcorn balls the size of golf balls.

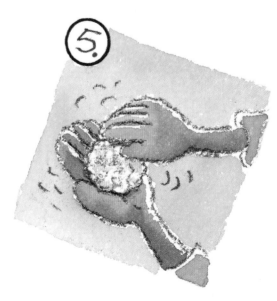

Sponge Cake to Decorate

Ingredients:

1 container (6 ounces) of plain yogurt

1 measure of oil (use the yogurt container for the measure)

2 measures of sugar

3 measures of flour

4 eggs

2 teaspoons of baking powder

1 Preheat the oven to 410°F.

2 Put the yogurt, eggs, and sugar in a bowl. Mix well with a hand blender or whisk.

3 Add the oil, flour, and baking powder. Mix well until you get a smooth batter.

4 Grease a baking pan with butter so the cake will not stick to the sides. Pour the batter into the pan.

5 Bake it for about thirty minutes.

1.

410°F

2.

3.

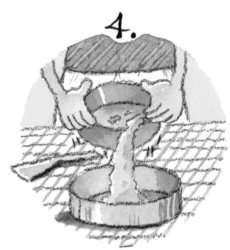

4.

5.

410°F 30'

Hot Dog Candies

Ingredients:

9 cocktail frankfurters

2 sheets of puff pastry

1 egg

kitchen string

You can also use a cheese filling for the candies!

1 Preheat the oven to 375°F. Pierce the cocktail frankfurters with a fork.

2 Roll out the puff pastry. Cut it into nine equal parts.

3 Place a frankfurter on each piece of puff pastry and roll it.

4 Pinch both ends tightly so it will look like a piece of candy. Tie them with kitchen string.

5 Line a shallow baking pan with aluminum foil. Grease it with butter. Place the "candies" in the pan and brush them with some beaten egg.

6 Bake for about fifteen minutes or until they look golden brown.

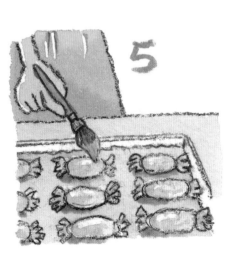

Mini Cheeseburgers

Ingredients:

12 ounces of ground beef

salt

tomato

cheese

lettuce

sandwich
bread

1 Add salt to the ground beef. Make small balls and pat them flat to make little hamburgers.

2 Fry the mini hamburgers in very hot oil until they are well done on both sides.

3 Use a glass to cut out round pieces of bread.

4 Place a mini hamburger on each piece of bread. On top of the meat, put a slice of cheese, a little bit of lettuce, and a slice of tomato.

5 Top the hamburger with another piece of bread.

24

If you leave the frozen yogurt in the freezer for several hours or more than a day, take it out half an hour before serving.

Frozen Yogurt

Ingredients:

4 containers (6 ounces each) of plain yogurt

7 ounces of whipped cream

4 tablespoons of lemon juice

3/4 cup of powdered sugar

1 Squeeze four tablespoons of lemon juice from a lemon.

2 Put the yogurt, lemon juice, and powdered sugar in a bowl. Mix it well.

3 Fold in the whipped cream, and stir with a wooden spoon.

4 Cover the yogurt mixture well, and place it in the freezer until it becomes as thick as ice cream.

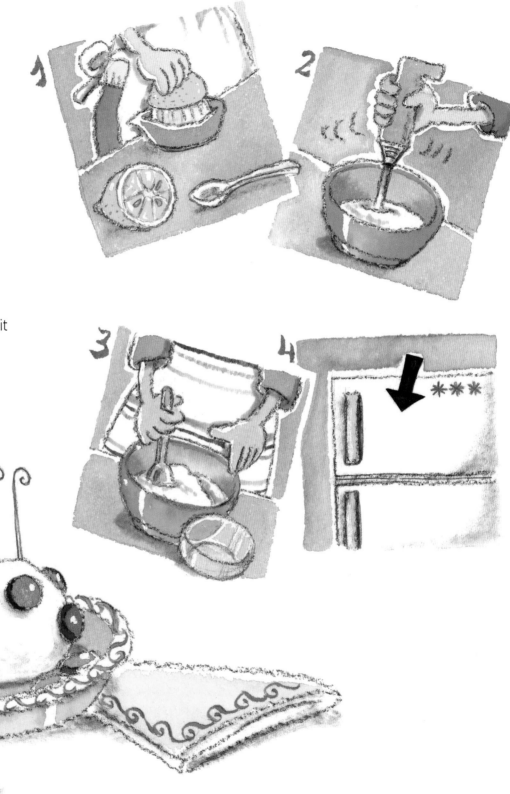

Fruit Shake

Ingredients:

2 apples

2 pears

2 bananas

2 oranges

2 tablespoons of sugar

*You will get
a thinner shake if
you add some more
orange juice.*

1 Squeeze the juice from both oranges.

2 Pare and peel the fruit before cutting them into small pieces.

3 Put the fruit in a tall container. Add the sugar and orange juice.

4 Blend with a hand blender until you get a creamy mix. You can also use a regular blender.

5 Keep the shake in the refrigerator.

Words to Know

roll in bread crumbs

scoop out

cover

boil

fry

pat to press

cook until golden

shake

place

brush

blend

sprinkle

Planning the Party

 Decide the date of your party.

 Make a list of people to be invited.

Send out the invitations. You can make the invitations yourself. Here is one idea for a design:

 Make a list of everything you need to buy. You may include snacks, such as olives or peanuts.

Think about the decorations you would like best: paper streamers, garlands, balloons, etc. You can make them with colored paper, yarn, pieces of candy, or any other material you can think of. Here are some examples:

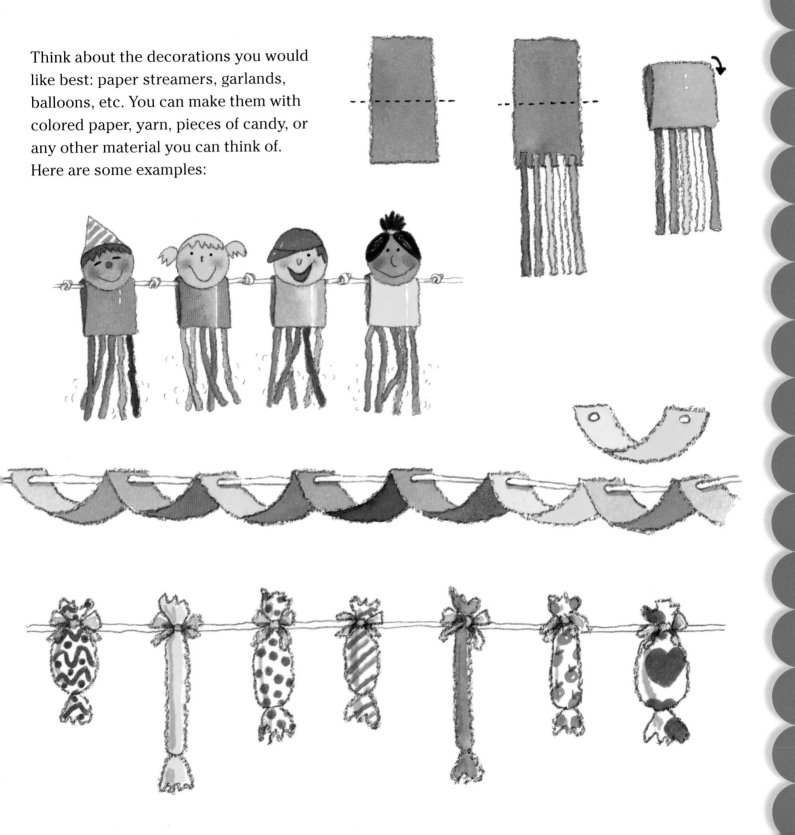

Organize fun games for the party. Here are a couple of ideas:

Pin the Tail on the Donkey

• All the party guests help draw a donkey without a tail.
• Each player makes a tail by cutting three strips of newspaper and holding them together with a thumbtack.
• Glue or staple the drawing of the donkey to a cork bulletin board.
• The players stand in line blindfolded and try to pin the donkey's tail where it belongs.
• The winner is the player who gets the tail closest to the right place.

The Flying Animal

• The players sit in a circle.
• When the game leader mentions a flying animal, the other players have to raise their hands.
• If a player raises his or her hand when the animal that has been said does not fly, or if he or she does not raise it when the animal does fly, the player will have to do what the game leader tells him or her to do.

Plan the party ahead of time. That way, you will not have to worry at the last minute. You can just enjoy a great day!

Read About

Books

Johnson, Kristi. *Peanut Butter and Jelly Sushi and Other Party Recipes.* Mankato, Minn.: Capstone Press, 2008.

Parrini, Sabrina. *Little Kitchen: 40 Delicious and Simple Things That Children Can Really Make.* New York: Skyhorse Publishing, 2011.

Time for Kids: Kids in the Kitchen Cookbook: 101 Recipes for Kids to Make! New York: Time for Kids, 2013.

Internet Addresses

Disney Family.com: Recipes for Kids
<http://family.go.com/food/pkg-cooking-for-kids/>

KidsHealth: Recipes and Cooking
<http://kidshealth.org/kid/recipes/>

Health Tips

Here are a few easy things you can do to stay healthy:

• Do not have too many sweets or sugary drinks, such as cake, cookies, and soda.

• Eat plenty of fruit and vegetables, and stick with whole grains, low-fat or fat-free dairy, and lean meats. For example, you can eat whole wheat toast instead of white toast or choose a grilled chicken sandwich instead of a hamburger.

• Eat breakfast, lunch, and dinner. Do not snack too much in between meals.

• Exercise every day. You can join a sport at school, take dance lessons, ride your bicycle, swim, jump rope, or play outside with your friends.

• Keep your teeth clean. Brush twice a day and floss. Also keep your tongue and gums clean. Change your toothbrush every three months. And see your dentist twice a year.

WARNING: The recipes in this book contain ingredients to which people may be allergic, such as nuts.

Enslow Elementary, an imprint of Enslow Publishers, Inc. Enslow Elementary® is a registered trademark of Enslow Publishers, Inc.

English edition copyright © 2014 by Enslow Publishers, Inc.

Original title of the book in Catalan: *FESTES INFANTILS*
Copyright © GEMSER PUBLICATIONS, S.L., 2003
C/ Castell, 38; Teià (08329) Barcelona, Spain (World Rights)
Tel: 93 540 13 53
E-mail: info@mercedesros.com
Web site: http://www.mercedesros.com
Author: Mercedes Segarra
Illustrator: Rosa Maria Curto

Library of Congress Cataloging-in-Publication Data

Segarra, Mercedes.
 Fun party food : little chef recipes / Mercedes Segarra.
  pages cm. — (The little chef)
 Audience: 7-8
 Audience: K to grade 3
 Summary: "Includes twelve recipes for party food, such as chicken nuggets, popcorn balls, and mini cheeseburgers, a 'before you start cooking' section, an illustrated vocabulary list, and party games"— Provided by publisher.
 Includes bibliographical references.
 ISBN 978-0-7660-4262-9
 1. Entertaining—Juvenile literature. 2. Parties—Juvenile literature. I. Title.
 TX731.S438 2013
 642'.4—dc23
                                    2012031116
 Paperback ISBN 978-1-4644-0467-2

 Printed in China
 122012 Leo Paper Group, Heshan City,
 Guangdong, China

10 9 8 7 6 5 4 3 2 1